CW00506474

Nina Parmenter

Split, Twist, Apocalypse

Indigo Dreams Publishing

First Edition: Split, Twist, Apocalypse
First published in Great Britain in 2022 by:
Indigo Dreams Publishing
24, Forest Houses
Cookworthy Moor
Halwill
Beaworthy
Devon
EX21 5UU

www.indigodreamspublishing.com

Nina Parmenter has asserted her right under the Copyright, Designs and Patents Act 1988 to be identified as the author of this work.
© 2022 Nina Parmenter

ISBN 978-1-912876-70-9

British Library Cataloguing in Publication Data. A CIP record for this book can be obtained from the British Library.

Designed and typeset in Palatino Linotype by Indigo Dreams.
Cover design by Ronnie Goodyer at Indigo Dreams
Printed and bound in Great Britain by 4edge Ltd.

Papers used by Indigo Dreams are recyclable products made from wood grown in sustainable forests following the guidance of the Forest Stewardship Council.

For David

Acknowledgements

Thank you to the following journals, blogs and presses who first published some of these poems, or earlier versions of them: Snakeskin (*Night Rails, Meanwhile in the Grasmere Conference Suite, STUFF, The Quantum Fox, Suffer-Bus, Photophobia, Something Else*), Fevers of the Mind (*The Twist*), Green Ink Poetry (*Araucaria Araucana*), The Wombwell Rainbow (*Blooming*), Atrium Poetry (*A Spell for Motherhood, Leftover Casserole*), Ink, Sweat and Tears (*Weak Core*), Form in Formless Times (*Squelch*), Selcouth Station (*Bone Ladder*), Dreich (*Thought Balloon*), Allegro Poetry (*Oxbow*), Lighten Up Online (*Lens*). *Dilton Marsh Walk* also appears at placesofpoetry.com, and some of these poems have also been posted on my blog at ninaparmenter.com.

A big thank you to Wendy Pratt whose courses and prompts inspired six of the poems in this book, and to Caren Krutsinger, Maureen McGreavy and Craig Cornish whose prompts led to *April Awakening, Ease in the Ether* and *Cracks* respectively. Thank you also to Colin Bancroft who gave me invaluable comments on a whole pamphlet-full of these poems. Massive appreciation goes to the many, many poets who I have met over the years online – whether on social media or on community poetry sites. There are too many of you to name, but your encouragement and feedback has been absolutely invaluable. And of course, thank you to David, Thomas and George for putting up with my constant daydreaming, scribbling and burning of dinners.

Finally, a massive thank you to Dawn and Ronnie at Indigo Dreams for believing in these poems and giving them a home.

CONTENTS

Split, Twist, Apocalypse

Foreword: Sense

I am a bag of chemicals
with charge for eighty years,
I am a gassy mirage
that winks as oblivion nears.
Around me swill the stars,
my thoughts, the gods and insanity,
and nothing makes sense but this leaf
as it dances, drunk on gravity.

I am a pointless voice track
on a puff piece for DNA,
I am the ooze that awoke
and decided to live anyway.
Around me swings the void,
nirvana and calamity,
and nothing makes sense but the sea
as it dances, drunk on gravity.

Heading to Martock

There is a time
in all our lives
when we are scared of
everyone
everything
but we find ourselves
in a van
on the A303
heading to Martock
with a friend
who wanted to see her boyfriend
who "was passing"
with his mate Dean
who only says
fuck
There is a time
in all our lives
when we are heading
to some party
at a moody boozer
in Martock
in a van
in a panic
in fact
we are always
heading to Martock
20 miles southwest
of our safe place.
Dean is driving.

Night Rails

At night, the trains roll in,
and I run the warp of the concourse
bagged down by luggage. Around me,
like the tracts of a living labyrinth,
staircases shift and flow.
Subways spread.

These are the same treads I chased
decades ago, when the rails bootlaced
the two sides of my life. But now,
I am a broken node, a traveller out of time,
tuned to the beep of the door buttons,
yet two beats afloat.

Some nights, when the points align,
the train doors open, and the dark
grants me a seat. For a moment,
we drive the lines together.
But the tracks soon curve
to steal my purpose, the signs
morph to hieroglyphs, and I am stuck,
hitched to my early adulthood, looping
from Coventry to Castle Cary,
destined only ever to change
                                    at Reading.

London Terminal

I lurch from the early train
unused to the lick of the track
and am hot-nosed into a coffee shop
with the wolfpack.

While the moon fades outside,
the blazered natives holler and lap
at great flagons of sharp-tasting black,
and I wonder if they're thinking of the void,
or fresh contracts.

So I ponder the list of coffees,
steamed or creamed, flaccid or flat,
and the cakes, like minuscule previews
of what life could lack.

And as the alphas stir and slurp,
I long to ask them how they wake each day and act
like they don't know this existence will retract
back down to a singularity; I mean
who wouldn't want to howl
about that?

But I whisper, "Latte please,"

and tuck my tail
behind my back.

Meanwhile, in the Grasmere Conference Suite

Mingle, they say,
and I feel stiff and spotty as a domino,
with a six at the bottom, dotted
in two tight rows,
and a one at the top.

Twenty minutes on the clock.
I take tea from the table
and mess up the twist-top milk jug.
I smile all down my straight flanks,
but curl inside.

Should I butt up to a wobbling single
or hover blankly
by a loose-set pair?
Will silence be my downfall,
or interjection?

I take more tea,
stage a toilet trip,
clank about with my game face
as if squaring for a match.
Fourteen minutes to go.

Eggs

Earlier today,
I whacked one in a pan to scramble.
A warm body could have bump-started it.
Which part of the yolk feeds the heart,
and which the magic?

Once, I stepped on a sparrow's clutch,
blue as the sky's long tumble.
A belly of down could have coddled it.
When it dropped from the nest like ballast,
did the albumin panic?

I spill a thick white,
I drop a spent shell into the rubble.
My fingers curl back at the waste of it.
I put a mic to my hollow abdomen
and hear the static.

Tubes

Here are some recipes for panic:

1   Speed, death, tubes, objects too close to the face,
the buying of gifts, high heeled shoes,
introductions.

2   Speed, death, tubes, big ambitions,
small space, committees.
The obligation to bake.

3   Speed, death, tubes, climate change, power,
the small amount that can be done in an hour,
the way happiness broadens the waist,
the word 'pension'.

4   Speed, death, tubes, ignorance,
toy soldiers glazed and grinning,
the world teetering like a coin spinning,
the size of the universe, the ten o'clock news,
time, distance, speed, death,
tubes.

Upon Reading That You Share 50% of Your Genes With Various Fruits and Vegetables

Now you understand
why you have always felt like a monkey's lunch,
a tangerine in primate skin,
fructose and peely pith.

Now you understand
why you were plucked and hung high to ripen,
why you grind like a coffee bean,
why you sprout,
why you seed.

You, with your new-found insight,
can shine like a half-melon moon.
You can blossom like a turnip in the earth,
half mauve.

Because now you understand
why you are so a bit of everything
that you cannot fit it all in,
and yet, you are always
half.

Of Course

We have both been here before,
my grandpa and I.
He, of course, was Napoleon.
I was a photon.

Like all the other Napoleons,
he had an empire to govern,
speeches to sharpen,
buttons to buff.
I had to be both wave and particle,
light-speeding like a spooked swallow.
Nothing in life is easy, child.

These days, over biscuits,
we talk about what it is to have changed.
But sometimes, we reminisce
about the curves of the ocean.

The Twist

I spin in my bed, my shoulders
pulled high and loaded,
the wings of my hips tucked
as if to fit some aperture.
I work rhythmically, arms
threaded round my ribcage,
my left calf cramping
as my feet close and flex.
My sheet shapes to my friction.

When it comes, it is inevitable:
my toe points a spasm,
my spine locks, and down I go,
turning through the mattress,
foamy swarf rising. Through and
through I twist, splintering
slats, scorching floorboards,
penetrating foundations. The soil
is a brief lick against my cheekbones

before the clay, the warmth,
the undreaming sleep.

April Awakening

In box-fresh spring light,
blossom sprigs quiver
and fringed leaves jostle –
unspeakably new.
My coy skin pinkens.

As clouds chuckle,
spine-cricks untwist
and songs teem free
to climb skywards.

Smiling, I
understand ...
all winter

I have
held my

breath.

Araucaria Araucana

It is spring. We walk to Robin Hood's Bower,
where low banks circle a herd
of fossil trees, necks stretched to the pale sky,
baying. There are no words,
just imprints laid on thick, dark air
that hangs in a hum of strips, sliced
by the crosshatched lattice of boughs
and the sacrificial rain of leaf-spikes.
The littered floor cracks beneath our feet;
a few well-worn stumps call
our eyes to their whorls of rings
and their snags of black sheep's wool,
while all around, willow shapes laced
with the blood cries of battles past
whisper of the things that fell
last night, when the runes were cast.

Robin Hood's Bower is the site of an ancient settlement in Longleat Forest, Wiltshire, reported to have been a gathering place for King Alfred's soldiers. A few decades ago, it was planted with monkey puzzle trees by the former Lord Bath, reportedly on a whim. This incongruous place is made all the stranger when you look more closely, and see the evidence of human rituals, which still take place there today.

Blooming

A celandine went first,
and if we had ever looked, we would have known
it was a freeze-frame of a live firework,
we would have expected
the violence that sparked from the inside out,
the heat petalling sweetly,
each stamen springing a hellmouth.

A rose caught,
thorns spitting pop-pop-pop from the stem,
the leaves crisping, and as an afterthought,
the buds, like charged kisses,
lipped the flames to ragwort and vetch.
An oxeye daisy burst,
white-hot in its eagerness.

We dialled nine-nine-nine,
but our words fell lifelessly away,
and as day bloomed into evening time,
the honeysuckle, its lashes
glowing in the last light of the sun,
tipped a long wink to Venus
and blew like an H-bomb.

Clearing Away

There are only so many times
you can unload the dishwasher
before magic happens.
It's down to the chink
of steel on steel, the spark.
It's down to the way light splits
in the bubble of a glass.
You will know when it is time:
deep under waves of rinse aid,
you will smell the earth.
Seize the spoon then, sister, seize it!
Make an arc in the kitchen sky
and say the word.

A Spell for Motherhood

Take a mountain. Scale the pink-arsed flanks of it,
limb over limb. Find Poseidon. Extract from him a wave
and a horse's hoof. Pluck a tree; kill the grip of it
by showing it your thoughts. Make your peace with the grave.
Eat apples, all of them. Taste in them the sin
of being a woman. Let that smack you in the gut,
you deserve it. Straddle the equator. Suck up its spin,
take it with you; feel your body snapping shut.
Learn to count each breath as an act of sedition.
Pull the lungs from a sleeping leopard. Be a speck.
Be a planet. Be a long-dead apparition.
Stuff a storm into your patch pocket, huge and wet,
but tell no one. Invent two new ways of shucking
a heart from a blown glass moon. Find a man. Fuck him.

Building My Baby

When the engineers had finished,
the electricians and the plumbers,
in streamed the tiny painters,
marbling vats of red and white
to make peach, rose and blush.

They took joy in their task,
frothing round the workspace,
washing my belly with song.
Work overran, but they assured me:
the tone would be exquisite.
The blending, masterful.

I couldn't wait.

Then, my son tore out,
all limbs, like a fat pink spider,
wet, black hair slicked to his head.
And the painters swilled out the red
in great, relentless bucketfuls,
leaving only white inside me
for a year.

Mother and Baby Doing Well

Nobody mentions
that you can feel like your baby
is a sentence,
that you might pray for him not to latch
so you don't have to bear it,
that your body is still falling from you
when they ask if you're feeling
normal.

Nobody mentions
that you might stand in the shower
and wish it undone,
or lie to a smiling midwife
because you can't not,
that advice feels like more fields to furrow
unless you are feeling
normal.

Nobody mentions
that a heart so hard pressed
cannot find rhythm,
that your tears every night
will wash you further from daylight,
that love does not come when you ask it,
or when they ask if you're feeling
normal.

On the Lip

I did not choose this body,
perhaps it chose me –
as driver, chef and skivvy.
I took on its sights and its flavours,
its knocks and its losses.
We'd go howling each Tuesday.

But my body has many endings,
bone-cricks and grumbles,
instincts dark and scratchy.
And my mind is slow-creeping lava
on the lip of an ocean.
The skittish waves watch me.

Weak Core

I have hauled laundry, sucker-punched Tuesday,
bent, switched and twisted,
and my spine despises me.
You have a weak core, she says.
Should be pulling up and in, she says.

Imagine a stuffed burlap sack half hanging
from a squealing sapling, the
whole massive hellish orb
on which we teeter exhorting it
groundwards. *Rip-snap*

and the pre-teen tree gives, bark
pinging like fish scales, fibre
parting from fibre, sap beading,
the unwieldy sack slumping
as Earth pops its nickel six-pack.

Wanna spot for me, sucker?

I do stretches, I say, take screen breaks,
eschew the hoover. I have
shiatsu balls. An orthopaedic mattress.
She laughs at the futility.
This way to the pulleys, she says.

Squelch

I heard the squelch of death again,
or was it just a neuron firing
deep within my boggy brain,

or possibly a cell expiring
under virus-spiked duress?
It could have been my heart perspiring

(that may be a thing I guess)
or, deep down in the adipose,
the squealing of a fat-lump pressed

to serve as fuel, and I suppose
it might have been a small mutation:
'Pop!' (we get a lot of those),

a bronchiole's sharp inhalation,
'Hiss!' a membrane's gooey breath,
a bile duct's bitter salivation ...

Probably, it wasn't death.

Bone Ladder

If I was belly-based, I could spend my days
sculling in lush pools of gut fauna,
warm and safe beneath my own flesh roof.
But I chose for my space the cranium, famed for its
panoramic views, its proximity to tongue
and tears, its sweet private access
via the top flight of the spine.

Each day, a billion stimuli send me scuttering
up the rungs of my neck, hot
as a bugged weasel, squashing seven skewed vertebrae
in my rush. And when there is danger –
a meeting, a journey, a decision –
I ratchet up my bones in painful panic,
retreat into the tissues of my tower.

Come nightfall, I offer my neck paltry thank yous:
seven hours, two squashed pillows, a mattress
made for the pain. And, quietly, as we lie there,
I apologise for my high-rise yearnings,
for the cruel toll of feet and gravity,
then beg it not to leave me, like Rapunzel,
scaling ropes of my own knotty hair.

Arrangements of Atoms

She is a fitful sleeper,
suspecting that when she wakes
she might be made of silica
or sadness. Arrangements
are not fixed, atoms make choices,
things that form can unform,
what's yours is hers, what's hers
is a cupcake. Half awake,
she thinks about covalent bonds
and free will and how it would feel
to be a cogwheel or an attitude
or a longed-for lover.
She tries mindfulness, feeling only
the pillow on her face, but then
the pillow IS her face and she is
whirling with skin and feathers
while the time until morning
is the skewed arc of a comet,
pulled by one body, then the next.

Dilton Marsh Walk

Today, as we skirt the bare field,
there is nothing but us and the sky
and the White Horse, nodding us by.

The soil is slick with the remnants
of the rain that we dodged yesterday.
The tracks of a dog mark our way.

Our fingers could touch a horizon
as wide as the yawn of the air.
The breezes lie quiet in our hair.

For a while, there's no family drama,
just four different sizes of boot,
each haloed with clumps of our route,
and the White Horse, in silent salute.

*A white horse is carved into the chalk hills overlooking the town of Westbury,
Wiltshire, and its surrounding villages, including Dilton Marsh.*

The Nursery

In the mud garden,
the courgette plant, spring-born and green,
makes a flower from yellow tissue paper
to take home to Mother,
then another, and another.

The flowers are too big of course,
too five-fingered to be real,
but the plant shows them off to the air:
the girl-flowers with their bald-headed babies,
the stamen-waving boys.

By the time Mother comes,
the flowers lie crumpled on the soil,
abandoned like so many small plans.
Mother hacks the babies free.
Uses them up in soup.

Ours

We give it a name,
we make it ours.

We claim the salt
that spikes the rock,
the gas that wakes,
the virus that breaks
the cell, the hill
that sweetens the view,
the milk that sweats,
the shudder that lifts
the ground, the sound
of cyclones that suck –
we give them a name,
we make them ours.

The crush of the snow,
the tang of the rot,
the horn of a hoof,
the lung, the tongue,
the moon, the shift
of grass in the wind,
the spider that tickles
the hair on our necks
and the words. The words!
The names that we give,
and the human delusion
of ownership …

There's a wheeze in the world
as it chokes on our words,
so we name it and make it
ours.

STUFF

STUFF trailed its tarnish across the Orient
then set out for a first-world future
like duped human traffic.

STUFF squatted in a whorehouse warehouse
waiting for empty shelf space, and the footfall
of an empty passer-by.

STUFF showed ankle in an email,
shoved its tongue in my High Street ear,
seduced me with sweatshop promises.

STUFF demanded its keep in energy,
whined for drawer space
and then crawled, feckless, onto my table top,
cheap plastic legs akimbo.

I looked it fresh in the eye and asked:
What do you want of me?
STUFF shrugged.

Viral Load

Round go the satellites
shining bright and benevolent, up
goes our space-junk shroud,
sixty silver dollars at a time.
On goes a slick of unity
to lubricate the press call, there
goes the glitter of war
in the back of an itching eye.

And here we are, so small in the telescope,
a sphere bristling with outliers,
poised to multiply.

The Sociopath Goddess Gives the Earth a Gift

I have stitched for you a pink jacket of humans
that does not fit, and honey, you totally own it.
When you wriggle your rocks, it's so cute! I'm assuming
you love the hot shove of the drill bit.
I blush as smoke rings and chaos shoot
from your stick-on collar and cuffs; I am touched
by the shrink of your jungle, the cringe of your fruit,
the deserts that spread like a headrush.
It's hardly haute couture, let's be honest,
but sweetie pie, couldn't you die for these men
who grease up your poles and make mince of your forest?
Oh honey. Don't worry! I'll fix you again!
I will pull your slack hands from those pink plastic sleeves
mouthing, "Hey, filthy guts, do you love me?"

The Quantum Fox

Have you seen the quantum fox,
the fox in flux, the paradox?
His whereabouts is rare, because
he's in his den and in this box.

This hokum locus tends to vex
the best of us; the mind rejects
the concept of his flightiness
as fiction or a foxy hex.

But fiction's just refocused facts –
a lens that bends, a parallax.
The fact remains that Foxy lacks
a fix, til someone interacts.

See, should you pry inside the box,
you'll find a fox, or not a fox,
and then this quantum nonsense stops
and everything is orthodox.

Because Everything Must Be Paid For

Once, a pied flycatcher flew past a Norse axeman
and in the flit of distraction,
the blade took the wrong tree.
A certain line of owls
met its end.

What might have become of those owls,
we'll never know.
But twelve galaxies, ripe to be seeded,
still twit-twoo into the cosmic wind,
their nightly calls

unechoed.

How costly do you think those axe strokes look
from the deck of an event horizon,
where each moment strings into the future,
revealing everything
that it will become?

Well, when the man on the edge of the black hole
totted it all up,
he seized in payment the gold thatch of Valhalla,
thought for an infinite instant,
then took a star.

Thought Balloon

She fluffs pillows and flails limbs
to beckon the night's silence,
but in vain. A small thought balloon
eases from her temple.

Now is the blooming time –
plans swell, regrets double,
the balloon's silk fills dizzyingly,
its nodding crown lifts.

Her basket rocks. Her stomach drops –
now is the soaring time!
The world expands and blurs.
Sleep tumbles from reach.

Her shoulders cling to her cheeks
as if bracing for impact.
But what does she think will break her,
except clouds?

November 27th

Last night, when the sky rattled the bricks in their mortar,
we gave her the shed door, begged her to play elsewhere.
She stirred at the roof-moss for a while,
laid waste to the bins that stood upright,
flicked a hemful of wet sleet from her dress coat
then dozed on the dawn's brief flare.

Today, she has spent the hours crowing,
geeing up the corvids as backing for her song.
And for the last part of the short afternoon,
she has darkened her wings, declaiming with her spotlight:
"Look at the trees I stripped! Are they not marvellous?
Look at the winter. See where you belong."

Leftover Casserole

As the schedule decreed, I had
leftover casserole for lunch.
I de-tubbed it sloppily and warmed it,
smelling yesterday
and the day before.

But even in the first greyish forkful,
the paprika had deepened,
the mushrooms had infused,
the meat had relaxed and softened.
My mouth thought it was all new.

When you came home, I kissed you,
noticing that you were more peppery
than when you left.
Later, over goulash, you pulled a new face
and I laughed.

Oxbow

We meet by the river
on a Wednesday lunchtime,
to the disapproval of your dry wife.

Sandwiches are eaten
from square lunchboxes,
and we talk about the shapes we used to make –
but not all of them.

"Do you remember," you say,
"how you used to come out with my words
before I'd even thought them?"

And I think about the river, and how,
when it curls round and finds only itself,
there is a reckoning.
A cutting of the slack.

Curated

In the back corner
of the museum,
a small acrylic case
with a copper plate
with a cursive font
that says
A HEART.
Due to my chest
no longer keeping time,
I assume
it's mine.

Suffer-Bus

Join me on the suffer-bus, she cried,
spraying mood-juice indiscriminately.
Come, take a bore-tour of my foibles –
I take payment in emoji!

The seats are the velveteen of my frustrated dreams,
the windows are bare-all panoramic,
and the night-black switchback bends
are psychosomatic.

There are packed lunches, she cooed,
feasts of failure and low-grade jeopardy.
Please, stick your straws deep into my flawed thoughts
and suck me.

The bus runs on a soupçon of self-obsession
lubricated by self-doubt,
and I, best pout forward,
will be on the mic
throughout.

Crabby

When she grows,
Crabby moults,
leaving her armour on the beach,
arm-casts like lucky sevens,
a pink pickelhaube shell.

See, she feels
the world's bite;
it is dirty, like lies that tighten.
So she puffs up, proud as a drunkard,
and she cracks.

Will you run
to her stub ends?
Will you scratch her shape from the flotsam?
Will you bend her leg-parts into crabby 'C's
and point them at yourself?

Will you perch
on her salt-plated back,
snip-snipping at her pincers?
Will you picture her shucked like a moist mouthful
and think of her taste?

In truth, she will not care;
Crabby is no meal for small fry.
She will be on the fresh side of the sea.
Renewed.
Sharpened.

Cracks

November. I am dancing
with the tree, as a storm
strips us down to the raw;
two old nest sites,
spent and pendulous,
ripe for a sharp frosting.

Scraggy to the bones
and half blasted, we
blow our scars open to the sky.
Ignore the rotting pretties at our feet,
we yell, gyrating.
We never liked them.

By January, iced bark is drooping,
and snowfall has lopped
our driest boughs.
Do your worst, Woodpecker,
we screech, as we twerk
through an arctic squall.

Ease in the Ether

"Reality is something you rise above." ~ Liza Minnelli

There is ease in the ether.
I am wrapped in ambivalence,
my mind a mercy of feathers,
full-fluffed and baffled.

Far above the flick-flack of tongues
and the dull tug of duty,
I cruise the dewy sky-trails,
watching the pedestrians

    lessen.

Wind in your twine, Earthman –
you would stick me like a scarecrow.
You would stuff me into your overworked shirt,
my wrists bleeding straw.

Pillowdrunk

The last thing you drank was tea,
it bubbles and stews in your centre,
the saucer swings, and you blend to
leaf-patterned fug. You see,
you're drunk on a breath of dark,
skewed by the puff of your pillow,
skin down to blood down to marrow,
heaving. Blankets start
to swaddle your offbeat heart,
snagging you safe for the journey,
but sleep doesn't come. Too early.
There's waves to ride. You are
red sand on a roaming dune
ready to scatter and fall,
a sailor with nowhere to call,
a fish in the cup of the moon
waiting to drown.

REM

I am your filing clerk
I drop corpses into your corridors
I can paralyse limbs
Ooh, spooky

Don't thrash, now
Nothing's real if you don't believe it
I can gouge mouths into melons
Ooh, toothy

Ordinary Jumper

on the morning
of your execution you
were in the kitchen
drinking tea in jeans
an ordinary jumper
took a phone call
from the ordinary air
they told you
they would not be snapping
your neck you would be
dangling three of you
six feet dangling
nine feet up
you would be
a fairground ride
soaps on ropes
in ordinary jumpers
we would stand
in the ordinary air
watching your six feet dangling
watching you squeeze and goggle
nine feet up
until you were all dead
dead jelly
in ordinary jumpers
dead ordinary
you took a phone call
they told you
it was cancelled you
were drinking tea in jeans
an ordinary jumper
we turned to face
an ordinary day
these things can happen

Fingers

If your mind leaves you,
reach the world with fingers –
ten, maybe more.
Splice them to every extremity.
No one can find them all.

Let them worm, keen and soapy,
through soft clay and gummy skies,
around rocks and peaks.
Let them seek out forms and changes.
No one can numb them all.

Be the sum of nerves and friction,
knowledge that has no grammar,
data locked in skin.
Your fingers will be your witness.
No one can blind them all.

Something Else

When I looked out of the window for the last time,
I saw that the back lawn had turned to water.
It must have happened around dusk.

It was not an ocean, dizzy with froth and salt,
it was something else, something as deep as a
man is tall; deeper in fact, so that the man

could stand unseen below the surface. Since dusk,
great skeins of dank weed must have bloomed,
because the water had a thickness to it, a slowness

like folded oil. I thought of the things I'd left
strewn on the lawn: my beach chair, my favourite glass,
the book I would now never finish. I tutted.

In the sky, dark stripes had formed
in anticipation of a rose moon. Oddly, the moon
was a no-show. The air hummed to itself.

Lens

Some things are easy to forget;
there's something about the curving sky.
We're sure we saw it once, and yet
these things are easy to forget.
A fleeting thought, a flush of sweat;
is it a lens, is that an eye?
But it's so easy to forget
that thing about the curving sky.

Photophobia

The light is like the sound of something breaking;
he waits inside the upturns of the waves.
Don't touch the switch. The click will find him waking.

The kitchen has the air of someone aching
to live. Reflections hold the things he craves.
Their light is like the sound of something breaking.

If light consoles you, watch the shadows shaking
in bedroom corners, cringing at his gaze.
Don't touch the switch. The click will find him waking.

I wonder, have you sensed a brightness taking
your vision? Have you felt in recent days
that light is like the sound of something breaking?

You may be free. I may be quite mistaken.
You could believe, for now, that you are saved.
Don't touch the switch. The click will find him waking.

It's time for learning darkness. Time for making
new plans, believing senses, finding ways.
When light is like the sound of something breaking,
don't touch the switch. The click will find him waking.

Dropping to the Right

If I hadn't been so unobservant, I might have noticed
that my heart was dropping to the right, causing blow-ups
in my spleen, that my children's trinkets were growing darker
        (flies, smiles, livers),
that the wormhole in the tall cupboard
was starting to smell like plasticine, and not in a good way,
that the roof was throwing off fossil-rich regolith.

If I hadn't been so placid, I might have been triggered
by the shutter-eyed bugs flashing indifference like underwear,
the tills ringing their victory bells across the village,
by the words in my mouth, the sand-coloured eggs in my hair,
the fact that the forest wasn't talking to me,
nor were my ancestors.

If I had been a little more lithe, I could have clawed
more time from the walls, then teased it into nunchucks,
I could have made myself small when the lizards came,
I could have gathered my two sons in my pockets and
        (reusable bags in hand)
ended my life as per the claims in my biography,
making my last stand in Matalan, queuing on the left.

The Committee on Rebuilding Concludes

And so it is decided:

The hummingbird will paint the sky blue
to show off her plumage, the fox
will stir the earth brown
with his forepaws and brush.
In the stream, the minnows will mix shades
of sand and heaven, while the trees
will draw the living green from the sun,
and later, its blush.

The toad will call in the spring
with her bubbled throat, the puffin
will tussock the clifftops
with sea pink and thyme.
The owls will colour Mars coral
until the stars come out gasping, and the bees
will fill the pollened air with purpose
as the hollyhocks climb.

We don't remember how it was before.
But this seems right.

The Last Word

As I wrote 'Goodbye', a crack appeared
before the 'D'. An 'O' fell in.
For a moment, I saw God.
He handed me a knapsack,
which was kind.

There were sandwiches packed, clean underwear,
a ticket to a bright new beginning.
I threw out the ticket, and caught the bus
to a place with no words –
especially not 'because'.

Unsurprisingly, once I'd alighted,
the 'O' fell from the sky.
I replaced my mouth with it
and gaped at my new freedom
in wonder.

Indigo Dreams Publishing Ltd
24, Forest Houses
Cookworthy Moor
Halwill
Beaworthy
Devon
EX21 5UU
www.indigodreamspublishing.com